MINIMAL LIVING

D1610753

BETA-PLUS

MINIMAL LIVING

February 2008
ISBN 13: 978 90 77213 92 6

CONTENTS

FOREWORD

Minimalism emerged in the United States in the 1960s. The trend for minimalism began in the field of sculpture and soon became popular with painters.

The development was less quick to take hold within architecture, but it was no less significant: architects inspired by minimalism, such as John Pawson, Claudio Silvestrin, Peter Zumthor and Alberto Campo Baeza, brought about far-reaching changes in the world of contemporary architecture and interiors.

The power of simplicity is fundamental to minimalist living: the purest essence of the home and interior, with no redundancy or frills.

This book presents fifteen recently completed projects by leading architects and designers who have been influenced by minimalism: they are all worthy ambassadors of the "less is more" principle.

Wim Pauwels

Publisher

p. 10 & 12-13

The kitchen and entrance hall in a house created by architect Alain Demarquette.

Kitchen design John Pawson and made by Obumex.

PART I

MINIMALISM
IN ARCHITECTURE

A MINIMALIST METAMORPHOSIS

This classic villa from the 1970s has been thoroughly refurbished and extended so as to satisfy modern living requirements.

The windows at the rear of the house were all rather small. Combined with the northerly position of the house, this created a rather gloomy atmosphere.
All of these windows were made higher and also extended downwards to floor level. A long terrace and balcony connect these spaces now; they lend a more varied appearance to what was a rather dull rear facade.

Inside the house, everything has changed. The entrance hall has a new layout and large pivoting and sliding doors provide a greater feeling of space in the various rooms. The hallway has undergone a real transformation, but the original staircase was retained.

Tall cupboard units have been installed in the kitchen to make the most of the limited amount of space. One of these units can be converted into an open-fronted bar cupboard. The floor and work surface are in flamed Pietra Piasentina. The tall table was installed by the owner and it serves as a breakfast bar and desk.

Pietra Piasentina has also been used in the bathroom and shower. The unit is in Corian. The taps are from the Dornbracht Tara collection. The highly polished mirrors were designed to increase the feeling of space in the bathroom.

HANS VERSTUYFT ARCHITECTS

Van Bréestraat 35
B-2018 Antwerp
T +32 (0)3 485 6762
F +32 (0)3 485 6764
www.hansverstuyftarchitecten.be
mail@hansverstuyftarchitecten.be

A DESIRE FOR THE ESSENCE

In consultation with the client, the architectural studio of Hans Verstuyft created a plan for the plot, the programme and the budget for this project.

The construction of walls results in new apertures.
Interior spaces are extended to the exterior of the building, and vice versa.
An outside wall has as much significance as an interior wall, and the same can be said of the floor and ceiling. The facade is not stylised or over-designed. Sections of walls and roofs are omitted where necessary.

The building gains expressive force through the interaction between inside and outside. What is not there was superfluous; what is there is necessary: a basic principle of minimalism.

The ground floor (with garden view) houses the rooms used during the daytime. The entrance is defined by the upper section of the building, and the hallway is the height of two storeys; this creates a link between the two floors, which is reinforced by the adjacent staircase.

The kitchen has a covered outdoor section; the dining room has light from above and it extends onto the patio, so the owners can dine outside by the garden wall in the summer.

One wall is missing in the living room: this section has been given over to the window onto the garden. The first floor has a multipurpose space and individual rooms. The terrace and the open sections through the building create a link with the ground floor. Ceiling-height doors connect all of the spaces.

The range of materials was limited in order to strengthen the look of the spaces. Each of the materials is in its natural form: rough concrete, dark wengé wood, plaster walls, naturally coloured aluminium. The entrance hall is the height of two storeys and has a large, high window that allows beautifully filtered light into the space. The kitchen, dining room and living room have a linear arrangement. They are separated by truncated wall sections formed by the kitchen counter and the hood of the open fireplace.

Leaving out sections of walls has made the windows in this property more than simple apertures. This creates a strong connection between interior and exterior: the boundaries are blurred.

The individuality of the materials was respected in the bathroom as well.

The freestanding bathtub is in flamed bluestone. The surface and the washbasin have the same finish. Taps by Dornbracht (Tara).

A frosted glass screen separates the bathroom and the bedroom.

HANS VERSTUYFT ARCHITECTS
Van Bréestraat 35
B-2018 Antwerp
T +32 (0)3 485 6762
F +32 (0)3 485 6764
www.hansverstuyftarchitecten.be
mail@hansverstuyftarchitecten.be

CONTEMPORARY LIVING IN HARMONY WITH COUNTRY SURROUNDINGS

The rural surroundings of this property formed the basis for the construction concept, with the nearby River Scheldt and the historical context also influencing the design.

Hans Verstuyft Architects gave a contemporary interpretation to these characteristics in their design for this modern home, in harmony with its surroundings.

The property was built around a traditional basic house structure, as specified by the local authorities.
Orientation, view, light and privacy all played a part in determining the position and size of the windows and doors that were inserted into the building.

The sloping roof has a traditional shape and is reminiscent of the natural and logical construction methods of days gone by.
The opening in the roof provides ideal light and ventilation (just as the hatch in haylofts used to) and even offers a view of the River Scheldt. The facade is built in locally produced hand-formed bricks and has been rendered to give additional protection, in the same way as farmers used to finish their exterior walls.

The unique, powerful colours of existing buildings were the reference for the colour scheme.
This approach ensures that a new building can be integrated into historic surroundings in a way that is both contemporary and authentic, without introducing any sense of fake history.

The long natural-stone surface in the living room serves as an all-round bench. Indirect light creates a variety of different atmospheres, depending on the time of day. Ceiling-height doors, specially made handles, stainless-steel hinges: all of these details reveal fine craftsmanship.

The custom-built kitchen is most suitable both as a workspace and as a dining area for receiving guests.

The base of the work surface and table is in stainless steel. All of the cupboard units are in white lacquer to create a contrast with the oak doors. Double doors link the entrance hall, the kitchen/dining room and the living room. These are a reference to the structure of old houses and their antechambers.

The same stone was also used in the upstairs bathroom.

The oak floor continues onto the staircase, which is otherwise finished in normal plaster, lending a simple and basic look to this part of the house.

The window on the landing before the top floor extends into the roof and offers a panoramic view of the River Scheldt.

HANS VERSTUYFT ARCHITECTS

Van Bréestraat 35
B-2018 Antwerp
T +32 (0)3 485 6762
F +32 (0)3 485 6764
www.hansverstuyftarchitecten.be
mail@hansverstuyftarchitecten.be

A STREAMLINED DESIGNER HOUSE IN THE UNITED STATES

Bruce Bananto is a renowned interior designer based in New York.

For this project, he worked with EA2 (European Architectural Antiques), an international company specialising in traditional construction materials from Europe.

The result is a minimalist mix of European and American style in a streamlined designer house.

Chairs and tables were designed by Richard Schultz in 1966.

The existing American colonial
fireplace was removed and replaced
with a minimalist porcelain wall,
supplied by EA2.

p. 46
Monochrome white
in an austere design
by Bruce Bananto.

The 18th century
Swedish Gustavian
writing table was
purchased through EA2.
Desk lamp by
Serge Mouille.

p. 48-49
The living room chairs
shown in gray are the
design of Gerrit
Rietveld. The white
opaque glass coffee
table is Italian. The pair
of white upholstered
chairs is the design of
Bruce Bananto.
A Hemp area rug by
Bruder of Antwerp.

The kitchen is a design by architect Bruce A. Wood of Boston (MA).

The chairs are by Italian designer Gio Ponti. Table designed by Bruce Bananto, made of Corian and stainless steel.

The dining table was designed by architect Bruce Bananto and custom built by EA2. The dining chairs are by Mario Bellini.

BRUCE BANANTO
>145 W. 28th ST.
>Suite 803
>New York, NY 10001
>T +1 212 563 1750
>F +1 646 416 6218

EA2
European Architectural Antiques
>26 Heistgoorstraat
>B – 2220 Antwerp / Heist op den Berg
>T +1 617 894 04 95
>info@ea2.be

HuntForAntiques.com
>4 Itegembaan
>B – 2580 Antwerp / Putte
>T +32 (0)477 56 03 38

A NEW HOME

This newly built house is the cosy home of a family with five teenage daughters. This decidedly modern and timeless building blends perfectly with its wooded surroundings.

The Reginald Schellen architectural studio prefers to work on projects such as this, where the aim is an integral approach to interior and exterior.
Light and space play a central role in the studio's designs.
Creating seamless connections between inside and outside is one of the studio's central credos: for this reason, interior architect Linda Coart was involved in the project right from the beginning.

The owner gave the studio carte blanche for the design and implementation. The designer has incorporated the client's wishes in this model of harmony between form and material, where functionality is always key.

p. 52-55

The house is rendered with crépi. Visitors pass under the floating beam in a dark crépi finish, then walk beneath a canopy to reach the front door. This 'outside room' offers a gentle transition from the outside space into the private home.

The recessed bluestone section and large corner window lend a floating impression to the upper storey.

The garden was designed by landscape architect Tom Caes.

p. 56-57
The transparent rear wall on the ground floor optimises the connection between the garden and the kitchen and living room. All of the windows on this south-facing facade have subtly integrated screens to keep out the bright sunlight and heat. The surround of the swimming pool is in large (1m by 1m) bluestone slabs that continue on to the terrace.

A great deal of care was taken in selecting the right lighting to create the ideal atmosphere. Features include LED lighting on the steps and floor spotlights in the entrance hall.

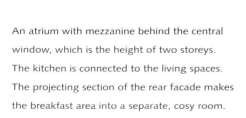
An atrium with mezzanine behind the central window, which is the height of two storeys. The kitchen is connected to the living spaces. The projecting section of the rear facade makes the breakfast area into a separate, cosy room.

This wide gas fire, together with the fitted compartments for audio equipment and the flatscreen television, is a composition in its own right. This integrated wall forms the focus of the living room.

The large open kitchen, which was designed by the architectural studio, has panels in dark-coloured oak. All of the latest technology is concealed within the walls.

The central block with its granite work surface dominates the room. This block extends to form a large breakfast table. The American refrigerator and cooker hood are beautifully integrated in a painted facing wall.

The home office on the first floor has a central position. The owner has another fine view of the garden from this space.

The sliding door leading to the wing containing the children's rooms disappears behind the bookshelves.

The white/grey oiled oak parquet floor blends perfectly with the parquet flooring downstairs and the wooden surface of the staircase.

In the parents' bedroom, we find the same parquet floor; dark-stained oak veneer in the suspended vanity unit and bath surround.

ARCHITECTS REGINALD SCHELLEN
Boslaan 26
B-2820 Bonheiden
T +32 (0)15 42 05 25
F +32 (0)15 43 31 37
MOB +32 (0)475 28 13 49
www.schellen.be
info@schellen.be

FUNCTIONAL MINIMALISM

In this project by the Pascal François architectural studio, minimalist design is combined with a very functional home.

This property has a streamlined appearance and radiates a sense of simplicity and calm, but this visual harmony conceals the very latest in technology and the ceiling-height wall units ensure an optimal use of space.

A view of the entrance, with a galvanised wall on the right that conceals a storage room. Above, a glass balustrade.

The photograph on the top left shows a detail of the skylight on the ground-floor entrance level. On the floor, an installation by the client, featuring old shoe lasts.

Top right, a photo of the guest toilet on the first floor. The washbasin is in concrete and stainless steel.

The bottom photo shows the concrete staircase from the ground floor to the upper storey.

A sliding glass door conceals the garage behind and makes the entrance appear larger.

p. 74

A view from the first-floor entrance hall towards the kitchen. On the right, continuous wall units with integrated lighting above. Behind these units are the cloakroom, storage space and kitchen equipment.

Above the open fireplace, a long strip in black fabric that conceals the music system.

p. 76
A view from the sitting room, showing the hallway on the first floor and the upstairs corridor on the second floor.

Top photo, a view of the closed cupboards behind the concrete kitchen unit; the photo below shows the appearance of these cupboards with the doors open.

The office, with a view
through to the living room.

p. 82

The upstairs corridor with an aged wooden floor.
As on the first floor, a continuous row of wall
units. The dressing room, washing area, part of
the bathroom and the stairs to the next floor are
integrated into these units. Front left, the stairs
to the office.

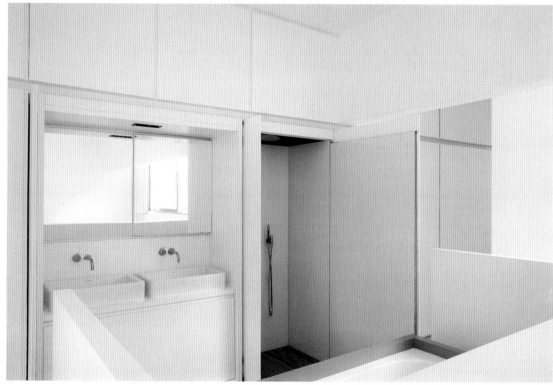

A bath with a U-shaped wall surround and details of the shower with painted glass.

PASCAL FRANÇOIS ARCHITECTS
Ledebaan 238
B-9300 Aalst
T +32 (0)53 77 66 98
F +32 (0)53 77 22 01
www.pascalfrancois.be

TRANSPARENCY, OPENNESS AND GEOMETRY

This recent project by Pascal François is a fine example of the virtuosity with which this architectural studio based in Aalst is able to create practical minimalism.

The result is an open living area, offering lots of garden views and with skylights and large windows ensuring plenty of light.

A view through the house from the entrance.

Front left, the black aluminium profiled sheeting of the wall cladding.

In the background, the glass walkway and skylight.

The entrance hall (with a frosted glass door leading to the bathrooms) and a detail of the prefab concrete staircase.

p. 90-91
The living room has a view of the two interior volumes. The block on the left contains the open fireplace and the daughter's bedroom and bathroom on the ground floor, with the parents' bedroom, dressing room and a second bathroom on the first floor.
The block on the right houses the kitchen, scullery, utility room, toilet and the concrete staircase leading to the son's bedroom.
A glass walkway with a black steel base joins the upper part of the two blocks.

The sitting room with a concrete desk unit in the background.

The cooking alcove with recessed cupboard units and a cooker hood.

A view of the complete living area: office, sitting room, kitchen and dining room unite to form a whole.

The kitchen is based around the same kind of concrete unit.

The bathroom with a walk-in shower and a concrete vanity unit on two levels: U-shaped and completely open underneath to allow wheelchair access.
The shower is clad throughout with square black Winckelmans tiles.

PASCAL FRANÇOIS ARCHITECTS
Ledebaan 238
B-9300 Aalst
T +32 (0)53 77 66 98
F +32 (0)53 77 22 01
www.pascalfrancois.be

THE IMPORTANCE OF LIGHT

The private residence and office of architect Pascal François is a sleek and simple brick volume, built in dark-red hand-formed bricks.

To accentuate the solid mass of the building, the opening for the entrance has been sliced away in an almost surgical fashion.
The moment your eye moves away from the brick facade, it encounters snow-white insulated plaster.

The southern facade of the house. Frameless windows have been installed; the windows that open have been accentuated and built in western red cedar.

The house as seen from the road.

A view of the private staircase with, front right, a work in glass by Anna Torfs.

Monochrome white predominates and has been used for the screed floor, the walls and the furniture. This choice accentuates the light in the house: daylight streams downstairs through the glass of the floor in the upstairs hallway.

This concrete staircase leads to the architect's design studio.

The open fireplace, a design by Pascal François, was created by De Puydt. The large glass window ensures that interior and exterior flow almost seamlessly into one another.
The ceiling in part of the sitting room is as high as seven metres: an important factor in increasing the sense of space.
Glassware on the small table by Anna Torfs, a family friend.

A "Jan" table in wengé by Emmemobili.
In the background, a white sideboard with two sliding sections that conceal a wengé interior and provide necessary storage space.

The kitchen has two concrete elements: the first is the U-shaped surround of the sink area, the second is the work surface in the cooking section.

A view of the kitchen and dining room, as seen from the sitting room. Once again, the glassware provides an accent of colour.

Part of the professional section of the house, with a view of the two meeting rooms.
A wengé desk, white lacquered cupboards and art by Achiel Hutsebaut, Pascal François's mentor during his internship.

A detail of the office with
Moon by Anna Torfs.

The design studio on the first floor.

Another consultation room. Right, a work on paper by John Zinsser.

Two levels in the flat roof, with a vertical glass window that allows daylight to fall indirectly over the entire length of the house: light is the key feature of this architect's home.

The master bedroom has a beautiful view of the garden.

The bathroom and shower are also bathed in white.

PASCAL FRANCOIS ARCHITECTS
Ledebaan 238
B-9300 Aalst
T +32 (0)53 77 66 98
F +32 (0)53 77 22 01
www.pascalfrancois.be

LIVING AND WORKING
IN A MINIMALIST SETTING

The home of architect Nico Verheyden and interior architect Carine De Hauwere is designed to connect in a minimalist way with the atmosphere of houses dating from the early 1900s.

The wide corridor with its ceiling-height double doors, the height of the ceiling and the use of symmetry and compartmentalisation in the layout of the house have their origins in the quest for traditional elements in architecture. The selected materials are also in harmony with this goal.

The ceiling-height doors in the hall provide access to the kitchen, the staircase and the living room. The view from the front door down the wide entrance hall towards the pool house at the back of the garden emphasises the depth of the house and the plot of land. The same ceiling runs throughout all of the rooms to maintain the continuity of the space. The floor tiles in mouse-grey concrete have been laid in both the interior and exterior spaces. The steps were specially made in the same concrete.

In the living room, the work Raven by Jacques Neve. On the staircase, an original panel of the renovated Atomium. The low chest was designed by architect Nico Verheyden.

The living room has a lye-treated oak floor. The ceiling is three metres high. The spacing of the double windows and posts is identical on the patio and garden side. The curtains have been designed as fabric shutters on a steel frame. The open fireplace can be closed off with a sliding glass panel incorporated into the wall.

The kitchen surface is in terrazzo. Other than the cooker, no kitchen appliances can be seen. A ceiling-height wall unit with pivoting doors serves as storage space and provides room for appliances. The walled patio can be reached via the kitchen and the dining room. This patio overlooks the trees in the park on the opposite side of the street.

The studio for architecture and interior design is
on the first floor.
The window provides a view of the space above
the entrance hall. The low bookshelves run as
panelling around the wall surrounding this
atrium.

NICO VERHEYDEN
Architecture & interior design
      Alfons Wellensstraat 19
      B - 2610 Wilrijk
      T +32 (0)3 827 11 86
      F +32 (0)3 827 18 52
      MOB +32 (0)475 999 516
      www.nico-verheyden.be
      info @ nico-verheyden.be

PART II

MINIMALIST
INTERIORS

A CONTEMPORARY INTERPRETATION OF THE CLASSIC *BEL-ÉTAGE*

In this project, architect Benoit Bladt and the Kultuz studio have created a 21st-century version of the classic bel-étage apartment, in which the living area is typically on the first floor.

Open spaces communicate vertically rather than horizontally, through the large window sections and open staircases.

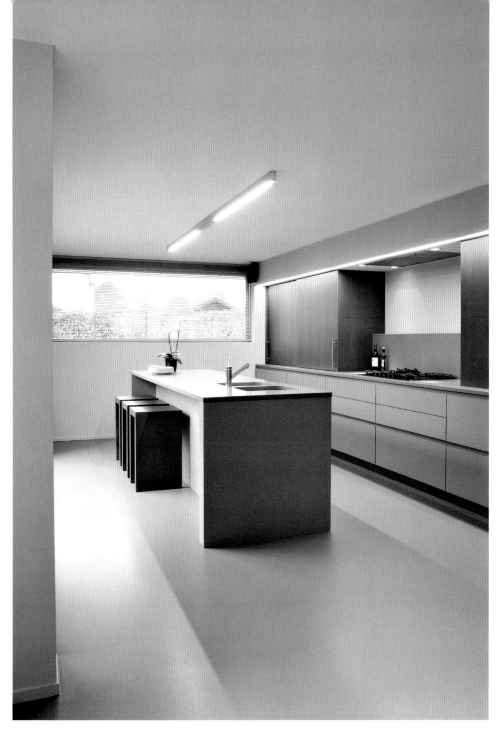

Kultuz designed the layout of the kitchen, which is architecturally interwoven with the building. The clean lines of the kitchen reinforce the sense of space, yet perfectly fulfil all functional requirements.

The red painted wall links the dining room to the living room and lends character to both spaces.

The decision to use under-floor heating removes the need for radiators and respects the sleek structure of the property. The glass balustrade around the atrium ensures fine views throughout the house.

The enormous glass sections provide a wealth of light, creating a fascinating interplay of light within this streamlined architecture.

The absence of joints in the screed floor and the simplicity of the bathroom and office increase the sense of harmony.

KULTUZ INTERIOR ARCHITECTS
Koningin Astridlaan 66 B1.1
B – 2800 Mechelen
T +32 (0)15 20 42 20
www.kultuz.be

BENOÎT BLADT
Architect
Franklin Rooseveltlaan 40
B - 1800 Vilvoorde
T/F +32(0)2 251 30 82
MOB +32 (0)475 27 08 05
benoit.bladt@cobonet.be
architectenbureau.bladt@edpnet.be

The open staircases, with no risers to the steps, allow natural light to flow deep into the house.

ART AND DESIGN
IN A MINIMALIST SETTING

This minimalist house was designed by Alain Demarquette, an architect from northern France, who was commissioned by clients with a passion for contemporary art and design.

Senior interior architect Kurt Neirynck from Obumex designed and supervised the home interior.

One of the most important sources of inspiration for this house was the Fondation Beyeler in Basel, a Renzo Piano creation.

Grey, white and black are the basic colours that recur throughout this project: this virtually monochrome palette ensures a streamlined and simple look throughout.

This unit in black metallic lacquer houses the storage area, scullery, toilet and cloakroom.

Design occupies a prominent position in this house in northern France. Concrete tiles were selected for the floor. The stairs are also cast in concrete.

The lines of the windows, which have been extended throughout the house, are inspired by Renzo Piano's Fondation Beyeler in Basel and they shape the architecture of this building.

The interaction between the interior and the exterior is very important here.

p. 144-147

Works of art by artists including Andy Warhol and Victor Vasarely in the open space containing the sitting room and dining room. Table by Le Corbusier and chairs by Knoll.

p. 148-151
The kitchen was created
by Obumex to a design
by John Pawson.

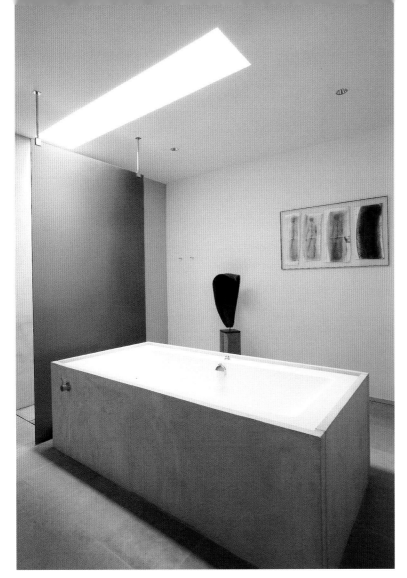

OBUMEX
Showroom Staden
Diksmuidestraat 121
B - 8840 Staden
T +32 (0)51 70 50 71
F +32 (0)51 70 50 81
Showroom Antwerp
L. de Waelplaats 20
B - 2000 Antwerp
T +32 (0)3 238 00 30
Showroom Brussels
Bd de Waterloo 30
B - 1000 Brussels
T +32 (0)2 502 97 80
Showroom Knokke
Sparrendreef 83
B - 8300 Knokke
T +32 (0)50 601 666
www.obumex.be
design@obumex.be

DEMARQUETTE ALAIN sarl
Architect
1 rue du Bastion
F – 59400 Cambrai
T +33 (0)3 27 37 87 84
F +33 (0)3 27 74 17 62
alain.demarquette@free.fr

SPACE AND LIGHT IN HARMONY

A young couple with three children built this luxurious house, together with Crepain Binst architectural studio. They called upon the services of 'aksent for the complete interior design. It was important that the clean, modern lines of the apartment should not become too chilly and cold. Stefan Paeleman from 'aksent took a contemporary approach that differs significantly from the normal designer look. The words 'past' and 'future' were important themes here. In line with the philosophy of their favourite design firm Promemoria, the link with the past ensures a sense of calm, whilst the future brings excitement and expectation.

In order to create a harmonious, yet lively floor, a parquet in strips was chosen, in wengé wood laid in broken bond. The walls have been plastered and polished, creating a natural effect that is calm, but not dull.
The large mirror and pouf are designs by Romeo Sozzi for Promemoria.

A stone washbasin by the toilet.

This semi-transparent sliding door in dark oak leads to the dressing room and bathroom and creates an intimate atmosphere.

Cloakroom in dark oak. Clever use of the mirror increases the sense of space. The glass of the mirror is slightly smoked to preserve the calm atmosphere of this space.

Colour and sophistication are the key themes in the living room. The chairs are in silk. Leather, bronze and precious woods also set the tone. The carpet is a combination of linen and silk. The curtains introduce a sense of casual informality. All of the furniture is by Romeo Sozzi.

Tall sliding doors with bronze handles separate the various spaces.

The library is one of the more closed-off sections of the house. It provides space for study and contemplation.
The red lacquer and dark-tinted sycamore are a reference to oriental cultures.

The staircase in blue steel and wengé has been left open so as to preserve a sense of space.

A multipurpose room for the children. The wall unit is an 'aksent design with doors in different colours to harmonise with the colour schemes in the children's bedrooms. Chairs: Poggiolungo by Flexform, table by Christian Liaigre.

The bar is the most funky and dramatic room in the house. On the bar is a work by Panamarenko. Mobile bar stools in stainless steel and leather by Karri Monni for Lapalma. Lighting by Bertjan Pot for Moooi.

p. 170-171
The fragile lines of this table and chairs clearly bear the signature of Sozzi. These are part of his Promemoria collection, all built in their own workshops. The lighting is also by Sozzi.

p. 172-175

The designers chose a natural stone for the kitchen that matches the materials used outside. The wengé doorframes create a link with the floors in the rest of the house. The cooker hood has been completely integrated into the ceiling so as not to form a visual obstruction in the room.

The table and benches are a design by Stefan Paeleman for 'aksent. Dark oak and bronze have been combined to make the table; the cushions on the benches are upholstered with a horsehair fabric by Le Crin.

The window with slightly smoked glass provides a view of the staircase.

Pale pebbles have been used for the floor in the children's bathroom. The insides of the cupboards are sky blue to create a holiday atmosphere. Three children: three sinks, with adjustable mirrors that can grow with the children.

The pebble floor continues into the shower. Walls in Portuguese sandstone.

A view of the wine cellar. This has been given a more rustic finish so as to evoke the atmosphere of the classic wine cellar. A table in oak and zinc (Philippe Hurel) and chairs make this an ideal spot for wine-tasting sessions.

The basement houses the relaxation space with a hammam, whirlpool bath, sauna, shower and swimming pool. The hammam and whirlpool bath are lined with marble mosaic. Floor in combe brune stone. The teakwood walls create a feeling of warmth. Recliners by Piet Boon.
The swimming pool has been lined with black pebbles.

A skylight in the bathroom allows in a wealth of light, yet provides the necessary privacy. Dark-tinted limewood is alternated with bronze and very pale "nozay" natural stone. The aim was to create a fresh and airy space that promotes rest and relaxation. Bronze mirror by Promemoria.

In the parents' bedroom, the natural stone of the exterior cladding has been extended indoors. This creates a sense of continuity in the architecture.

'Aksent
Interior Architecture
      Hoogpoort 43-45
      B – 9000 Gent
      T +32 (0)9 225 71 66
      F +32 (0)9 225 02 67
      www.taksent.be
      info@taksent.be

FIREPLACES MADE TO ORDER

The family firm De Puydt has been setting trends in contemporary interiors with its open fireplaces for thirty years. These fireplaces combine the pleasure of brilliant design with the assurance of modern technology.

De Puydt's fireplaces are professionally installed by company-trained specialists, on the basis of a precise work plan and an agreed budget.

Visitors can discover the unlimited possibilities of an open fireplace at De Puydt's large showrooms, where over forty different arrangements are on display, including wall-mounted fireplaces, corner pieces and units that are open on three sides. All of the models are available in different sizes and can be made to order. Experienced interior architects are happy to advise the client about installation and matching furniture.

p. 188-191

A gas fire in a house designed by architect Marc Corbiau.

p. 192-195

A gas fireplace was selected for this house with a minimalist design.

This wood-burner has been seamlessly integrated into a contemporary interior.

DE PUYDT

Mariakerksesteenweg 197
9031 Drongen
T +32 (0)9 226 25 01
F +32 (0)9/ 227 93 21

Natiënlaan 215
B – 8300 Knokke
T +32 (0)50 34 24 44
F +32 (0)50 33 67 60

www.depuydthaarden.be
info@depuydthaarden.be

ADDRESSES

p. 198-200

An interior project by Kultuz in a house designed by Benoît Bladt.

'AKSENT
Interior Architecture
Hoogpoort 43-45
B – 9000 Gent
T +32 (0)9 225 71 66
F +32 (0)9 225 02 67
www.taksent.be
info@taksent.be
p. 158-187

BRUCE BANANTO
145 W. 28th ST.
Suite 803
New York, NY 10001
T +1 212 563 1750
F +1 646 416 6218
p. 44-51

BENOIT BLADT
Architect
Franklin Rooseveltlaan 40
B - 1800 Vilvoorde
T/F +32(0)2 251 30 82
MOB +32 (0)475 27 08 05
benoit.bladt@cobonet.be
architectenbureau.bladt@edpnet.be
p. 128-137

DEMARQUETTE ALAIN sarl
Architect
1 rue du Bastion
F – 59400 Cambrai
T +33 (0)3 27 37 87 84
F +33 (0)3 27 74 17 62
alain.demarquette@free.fr
p. 138-157

DE PUYDT nv
Mariakerksesteenweg 197
9031 Drongen
T +32 (0)9 226 25 01
F +32 (0)9/ 227 93 21
Natiënlaan 215
B – 8300 Knokke
T +32 (0)50 34 24 44
F +32 (0)50 33 67 60
www.depuydthaarden.be
info@depuydthaarden.be
p. 188-197

EA2
European Architectural Antiques
26 Heistgoorstraat
B – 2220 Antwerpen / Heist op den Berg
T +1 617 894 04 95
info@ea2.be
p. 44-51

PASCAL FRANCOIS ARCHITECTS bvba
Ledebaan 238
B-9300 Aalst
T +32 (0)53 77 66 98
F +32 (0)53 77 22 01
www.pascalfrancois.be
p. 72-115

HuntForAntiques.com
4 Itegembaan
B – 2580 Antwerpen / Putte
T +32 (0)477 56 03 38
p. 44-51

KULTUZ INTERIOR ARCHITECTS

Koningin Astridlaan 66 B1.1

B – 2800 Mechelen

T +32 (0)15 20 42 20

www.kultuz.be

p. 128-137

OBUMEX

Showroom Staden

Diksmuidestraat 121

B - 8840 Staden

T +32 (0)51 70 50 71

F +32 (0)51 70 50 81

Showroom Antwerp

L. de Waelplaats 20

B - 2000 Antwerp

T +32 (0)3 238 00 30

Showroom Brussels

Bd de Waterloo 30

B - 1000 Brussels

T +32 (0)2 502 97 80

Showroom Knokke

Sparrendreef 83

B - 8300 Knokke

T +32 (0)50 601 666

www.obumex.be

design@obumex.be

p. 138-157

REGINALD SCHELLEN ARCHITECTS

Boslaan 26

B-2820 Bonheiden

T +32 (0)15 42 05 25

F +32 (0)15 43 31 37

MOB +32 (0)475 28 13 49

www.schellen.be

info@schellen.be

p. 52-71

NICO VERHEYDEN

Architecture & Interior Design

Alfons Wellensstraat 19

B - 2610 Wilrijk

T +32 (0)3 827 11 86

F +32 (0)3 827 18 52

MOB +32 (0)475 999 516

www.nico-verheyden.be

info @ nico-verheyden.be

p. 116-125

HANS VERSTUYFT ARCHITECTS

Van Bréestraat 35

B-2018 Antwerpen

T +32 (0)3 485 6762

F +32 (0)3 485 6764

www.hansverstuyftarchitecten.be

mail@hansverstuyftarchitecten.be

p. 16-43

PUBLISHER

BETA-PLUS Publishing

Termuninck 3

B - 7850 Enghien (Belgium)

T +32 (0)2 395 90 20

F +32 (0)2 395 90 21

www.betaplus.com

info@betaplus.com

PHOTOGRAPHY

All pictures: Jo Pauwels

GRAPHIC DESIGN

POLYDEM

Nathalie Binart

TRANSLATION

Laura Watkinson

February 2008

ISBN 13: 978 90 77213 92 6